I0843227

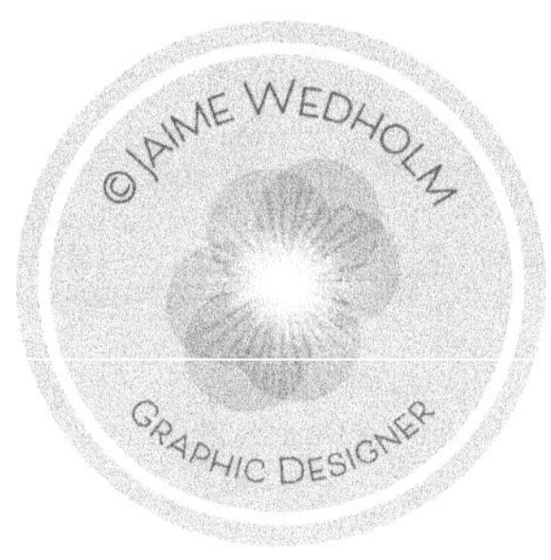

Copyright © 2019 by Jaime Wedholm

All rights reserved.

No part of this book may be reproduced, distributed or transmitted in any form or by any means, electronic or mechanical, including scanning, electronic sharing, photocopying, or by any information storage and retrieval system, without the prior written permission from the publisher and copyright owner, except for the review for inclusion in a magazine, blog, newspaper or broadcast.

For more information please contact: info@jwedholmdesign.ca

First paperback edition October 2019.

Book design & illustrations by Jaime Wedholm.

ISBN 9781694657053 (Amazon paperback)

www.jwedholmdesign.ca/shop

ACKNOWLEDGMENTS

To my fans – may you find joy in colouring this collection of designs!

To my champions who encourage and cheer me on from the
sidelines, I love you and treasure your amazing support.

Special mention to my talented team of colourists, each of whom have a wonderful
and unique colouring style. I am so grateful to this group of ladies for sharing
their coloured pages in the online colouring community, and helping to build
awareness of my books. Their gracious support means the world to me.

Vicki Ardito

Alina Bucur

Debbie West Cummings

Brittany Dobbins

Sarah Goode

Beth Lahna Haskell

Tina Helzer

Cari McBroom Jimenez

Stephanie Endicott Kalinec

Tiffany Kleinsteuber

Angie Mitchell

Emma Parkinson

Kelsey Ross

Donna Sugra

Christina Workman

Please join the fun and share your beautifully coloured pages in my
Facebook Fan Group @ **www.fb.com/groups/SipColourSmile**
It warms my heart to see your posts!

Happy Colouring!

CLAIM YOUR FREE
PDF COPY OF *THE REFILL!*

That's right!
As a THANK YOU for purchasing the paperback, I am gifting you a FREE pdf
download of this entire book that you can print and enjoy forever and ever!

CLAIM IT NOW BY VISITING:

JWedholmDesign.ca/the-refill-download

*PDF download is for personal use only
– NOT for distribution or commercial resale.

© 2019 *Sip Colour Smile: THE REFILL* by Jaime Wedholm
More at JWedholmDesign.ca/SHOP

© 2019 *Sip Colour Smile: THE REFILL* by Jaime Wedholm
More at JWedholmDesign.ca/SHOP

© 2019 *Sip Colour Smile: THE REFILL* by Jaime Wedholm
More at JWedholmDesign.ca/SHOP

© 2019 *Sip Colour Smile: THE REFILL* by Jaime Wedholm
More at JWedholmDesign.ca/SHOP

© 2019 *Sip Colour Smile: THE REFILL* by Jaime Wedholm
More at JWedholmDesign.ca/SHOP

© 2019 *Sip Colour Smile: THE REFILL* by Jaime Wedholm

More at JWedholmDesign.ca/SHOP

© 2019 *Sip Colour Smile: THE REFILL* by Jaime Wedholm
More at JWedholmDesign.ca/SHOP

© 2019 *Sip Colour Smile: THE REFILL* by Jaime Wedholm
More at JWedholmDesign.ca/SHOP

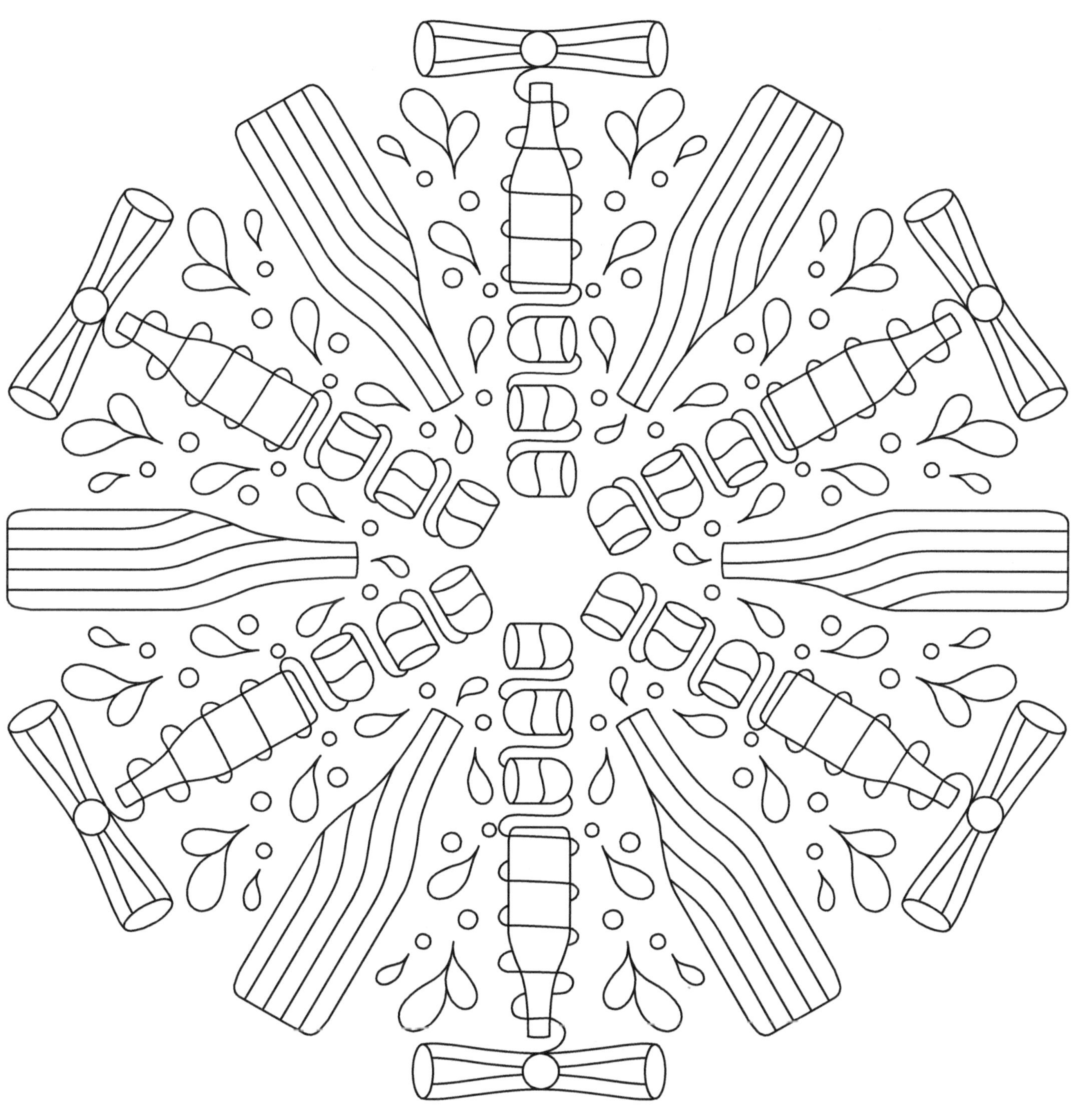

© 2019 *Sip Colour Smile: THE REFILL* by Jaime Wedholm
More at JWedholmDesign.ca/SHOP

© 2019 *Sip Colour Smile: THE REFILL* by Jaime Wedholm
More at JWedholmDesign.ca/SHOP

© 2019 *Sip Colour Smile: THE REFILL* by Jaime Wedholm
More at JWedholmDesign.ca/SHOP

© 2019 *Sip Colour Smile: THE REFILL* by Jaime Wedholm
More at JWedholmDesign.ca/SHOP

© 2019 *Sip Colour Smile: THE REFILL* by Jaime Wedholm

More at JWedholmDesign.ca/SHOP

© 2019 *Sip Colour Smile: THE REFILL* by Jaime Wedholm
More at JWedholmDesign.ca/SHOP

© 2019 *Sip Colour Smile: THE REFILL* by Jaime Wedholm
More at JWedholmDesign.ca/SHOP

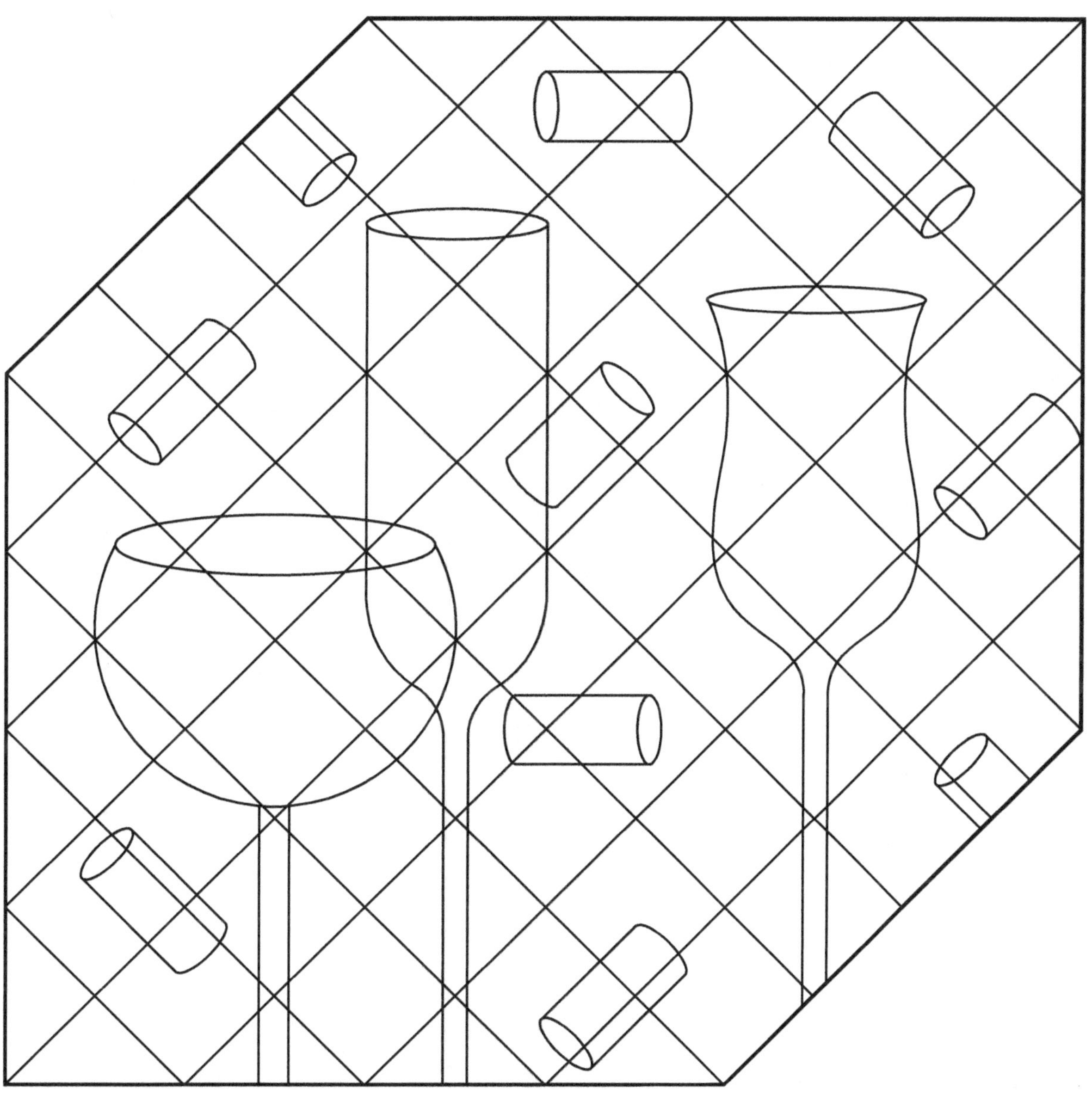

© 2019 *Sip Colour Smile: THE REFILL* by Jaime Wedholm
More at JWedholmDesign.ca/SHOP

© 2019 *Sip Colour Smile: THE REFILL* by Jaime Wedholm
More at JWedholmDesign.ca/SHOP

© 2019 *Sip Colour Smile: THE REFILL* by Jaime Wedholm
More at JWedholmDesign.ca/SHOP

© 2019 *Sip Colour Smile: THE REFILL* by Jaime Wedholm
More at JWedholmDesign.ca/SHOP

© 2019 *Sip Colour Smile: THE REFILL* by Jaime Wedholm
More at JWedholmDesign.ca/SHOP

BOOKMARKS ARE A FUN KEEPSAKE!

Colour, cut them out, laminate and enjoy for as long as you wish.

© 2019 *Sip Colour Smile: THE REFILL* by Jaime Wedholm

More at JWedholmDesign.ca/SHOP

BOOKMARKS ARE A FUN KEEPSAKE!

Colour, cut them out, laminate and enjoy for as long as you wish.

© 2019 *Sip Colour Smile: THE REFILL* by Jaime Wedholm
More at JWedholmDesign.ca/SHOP

COLOUR PALETTE TEST PAGE

Use this page to test and play around with colour swatches and combinations.

COLOUR PALETTE TEST PAGE

Use this page to test and play around with colour swatches and combinations.

COLOUR PALETTE TEST PAGE

Use this page to test and play around with colour swatches and combinations.

COLOUR PALETTE TEST PAGE

Use this page to test and play around with colour swatches and combinations.

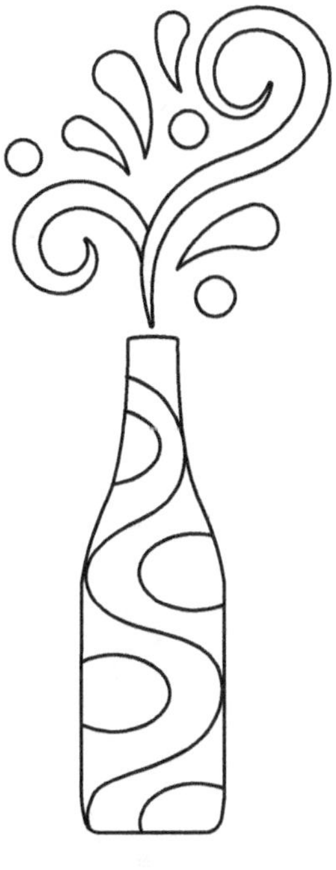

www.ingramcontent.com/pod-product-compliance
Lightning Source LLC
Chambersburg PA
CBHW081601270726
48657CB00029B/3455